HE **SAID**
SHE SAID

Men and Women
Square Off on Sex,
Money, and
Who Rules the World

By the Editors of **skirt!**® Magazine

skirt!

An Imprint of The Globe Pequot Press
GUILFORD, CONNECTICUT

To buy books in quantity for corporate use
or incentives, call **(800) 962–0973**
or e-mail **premiums@GlobePequot.com**.

skirt!® is an imprint of The Globe Pequot Press.

skirt! is a registered trademark of Morris Publishing Group, LLC, and is used
with express permission.

10 9 8 7 6 5 4 3 2

Printed in the U.S.A.

Designed by Diana Nuhn
Cover design by Diana Nuhn

Library of Congress Cataloging-in-Publication Data is available.
ISBN: 978-1-59921-291-3

skirt!

skirt!® is an attitude . . . spirited, independent, outspoken, serious, playful and irreverent, sometimes controversial, always passionate.

Contents

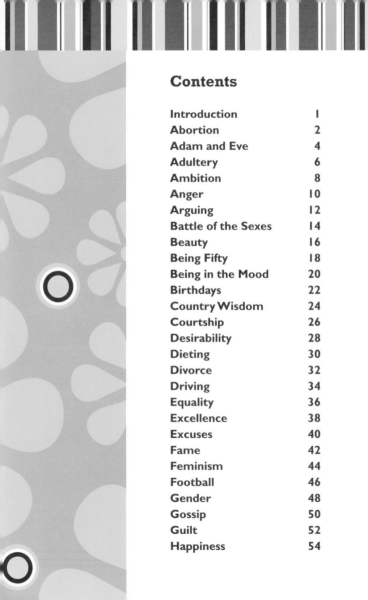

Introduction	1
Abortion	2
Adam and Eve	4
Adultery	6
Ambition	8
Anger	10
Arguing	12
Battle of the Sexes	14
Beauty	16
Being Fifty	18
Being in the Mood	20
Birthdays	22
Country Wisdom	24
Courtship	26
Desirability	28
Dieting	30
Divorce	32
Driving	34
Equality	36
Excellence	38
Excuses	40
Fame	42
Feminism	44
Football	46
Gender	48
Gossip	50
Guilt	52
Happiness	54

Heaven	56
Housework	58
Identity	60
Leadership	62
Love	64
Luck	66
Marriage	68
Men	70
Money	72
Monogamy	74
Passion	76
Peace	78
Penis Envy	80
Politics	82
Power	84
Pregnancy	86
Problem Solving	88
Rivalry	90
Ruling the World	92
Sex	94
Shoes	96
Success	98
Taking Risks	100
Travel	102
Walking	104
Wives	106
Women	108
Work	110

Introduction

Whenever a man has something to say, you can be sure a woman always has to have the last word . . .

Men and women have been trying to get in the last word since the first argument about who offered whom the apple. (At skirt!, we have our own opinion on that.) Despite thousands of years and thousands of self-help books, the conversation goes on and on and on—often contentious, sometimes deadly, but never dull! From bedrooms and boardrooms to divorce courts and cocktail parties, the parry and thrust of an incisive quip will be countered by a bludgeoning put-down. At other times, men and women will arrive at the same conclusion via very different and diverting routes. There's nothing more satisfying than a clever riposte, and we have to admire that whether it comes from a man or a woman. We've been collecting our favorite examples at skirt! for a long time, and we hope this collection will make you laugh or say ah ha! . . . and maybe even give you a snappy comeback for your next match of wits.

—Nikki Hardin, Publisher, skirt! magazine

he said

"I will do everything in my power to restrict abortion."

—George W. Bush,
President of the United States

"Abortion is not a presidential matter. Education is the answer. Morals cannot be legislated."

—Barbara Bush, former First Lady and mother to George W. Bush

He Said:

"I've learned a lot about women. I think I've learned exactly how the fall of man occurred in the Garden of Eden. Adam and Eve were in the Garden of Eden, and Adam said one day, 'Wow, Eve, here we are, at one with nature, at one with God, we'll never age, we'll never die, and all our dreams come true the instant that we have them.' And Eve said, 'Yeah ... it's just not enough is it?'"
—Bill Hicks, Comedian

She Said:

"God made man and then said: I can do better than that and made woman."
—Adele Rogers St. Johns, writer

4 On Adam and Eve

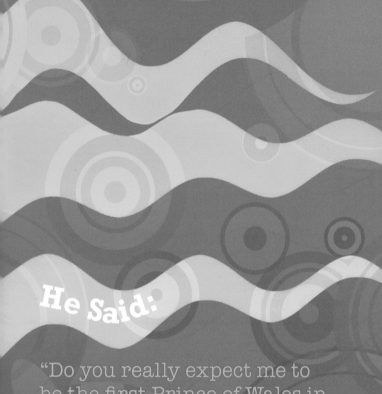

He Said:

"Do you really expect me to be the first Prince of Wales in history not to have a mistress?"

—Prince Charles, heir to the British throne

She said:

"My attitude toward men who mess around is simple: If you find 'em, kill 'em."

—Loretta Lynn, songwriter and musician

He Said:

"If any of my competitors were drowning, I'd stick a hose in their mouth."

—Ray Kroc,
founder of McDonald's

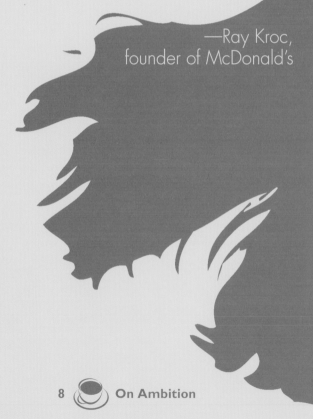

On Ambition

She Said:

"Don't
fuck with
me, fellas.
This ain't my first
time at the rodeo."

—Joan Crawford, actress

He Said:

"Don't get mad, get even."
—Joseph P. Kennedy, statesman

She Said:

"Don't get mad, get everything."

—Ivana Trump,
hotelier and entrepreneur

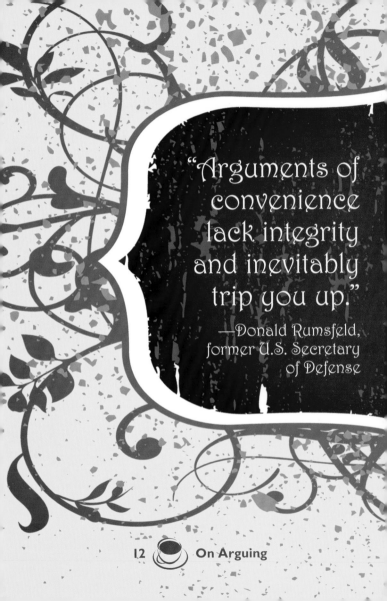

"Arguments of convenience lack integrity and inevitably trip you up."

—Donald Rumsfeld, former U.S. Secretary of Defense

"Fear not those who argue but those who dodge."
—Marie Ebner-Eschenbach, author

He Said:

"Nobody will ever win the Battle of the Sexes. There's just too much fraternizing with the enemy."

—Henry Kissinger, former U.S. Secretary of State

"Men weren't really the enemy; they were fellow victims suffering from an outmoded masculine mystique that made them feel unnecessarily inadequate when there were no bears to kill."

—Betty Friedan, activist and writer

He Said:

"A woman's beauty is one of her great missions."
—Richard Le Gallienne, author and literary critic

She Said:

"Beauty, to me, is about being comfortable in your own skin; that, or a kick-ass red lipstick."
—Gwyneth Paltrow, actress

He Said:

"At age fifty, everyone
has the face he deserves."

—George Orwell, author

She Said:

"Looking fifty is great—if you're sixty."
—Joan Rivers, comedian

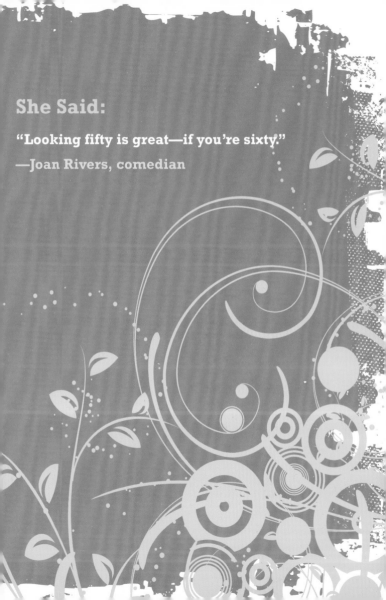

He Said:

"Women need a reason to have sex. Men just need a place."

—Billy Crystal, comedian

"Don't cook.
Don't clean.
No man will ever
make love to a
woman because she
waxed the linoleum—
'My God, the floor's
immaculate. Lie down,
you hot bitch.'"

—**Joan Rivers, comedian**

he said

"A diplomat is a man who always remembers a woman's birthday but never remembers her age."

—Robert Frost, poet

"A man who correctly guesses a woman's age may be smart, but he's not very bright."

—Lucille Ball, comedian

"Having a lot of horse sense doesn't keep a man from acting like a jackass."

—Sam Rayburn,
former U.S. Representative from Texas

She Said:

"The roosters may crow but the hens deliver the goods."

—Ann Richards,
former governor of Texas

he said

"Those marriages generally abound most with love and constancy that are preceded by a long courtship."

—Joseph Addison, author

she said "A lady's imagination is very rapid; it jumps from admiration to love, from love to matrimony in a moment."

~Jane Austen, author

He Said:

"Only God, my dear, could love you for yourself alone and not your yellow hair."

—W. B. Yeats, poet

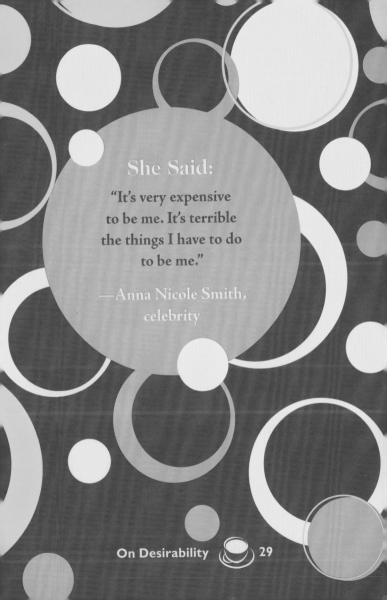

She Said:

"It's very expensive
to be me. It's terrible
the things I have to do
to be me."

—Anna Nicole Smith,
celebrity

He Said:

"To lengthen thy life, lessen thy meals."
—Benjamin Franklin, statesman, author, and inventor

She Said:

"The only time to eat diet food is while you're waiting for the steak to cook."
—Julia Child, chef, author, and television personality

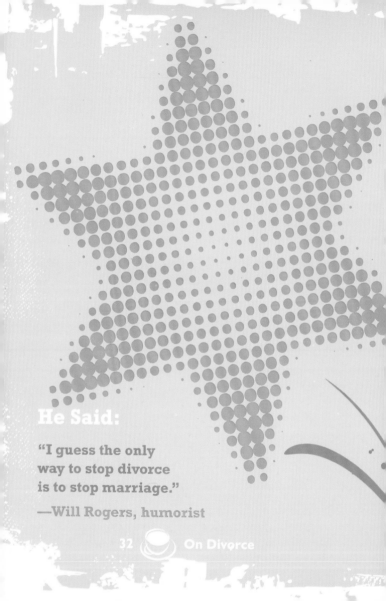

He Said:

"I guess the only
way to stop divorce
is to stop marriage."

—Will Rogers, humorist

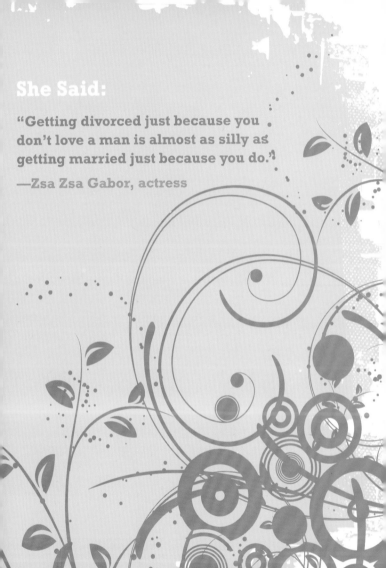

She Said:

"Getting divorced just because you don't love a man is almost as silly as getting married just because you do."

—Zsa Zsa Gabor, actress

"If your wife wants to learn to drive, don't stand in her way."

—Sam Levenson, radio and television personality

"I like to drive
with my knees.
Otherwise, how
can I put on my
lipstick and talk
on the phone?"
—Sharon Stone, actress

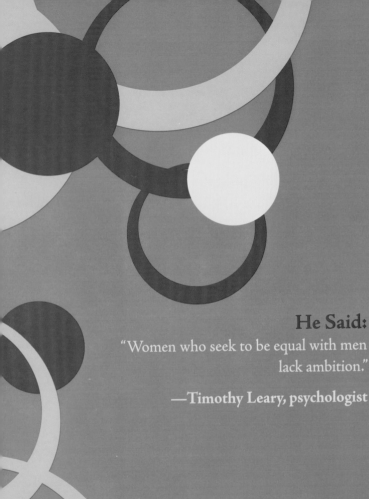

He Said:

"Women who seek to be equal with men
lack ambition."

—Timothy Leary, psychologist

She Said:

"A woman who thinks she is intelligent demands the same rights as a man; an intelligent woman gives up."

—Sidonie-Gabrielle Colette, author

he said

"One of the rarest things that a man ever does is to do the best he can."

—Josh Billings, humorist

On Excellence

"Whatever women do they must do twice as well as men to be thought half as good. Luckily, this is not difficult."

—Charlotte Whitton,
former mayor of Ottawa,
Ontario, Canada

he said

"*Fiction was invented the day that Jonah arrived home and told his wife that he was three days late because he had been swallowed by a whale.*"

—Gabriel García Márquez, author

she said "We need to bear the excuses men make to themselves for their worthlessness." —Margaret Fuller, writer and editor

He Said:

"It is strange to be known
so universally and yet
to be so lonely."

—Albert Einstein,
scientist and
Nobel Laureate

She Said:

"I don't think I realized the cost of fame is that it's open season on every moment of your life."

—Julia Roberts, actress

He Said:

"Feminism encourages women to leave their husbands, kill their children, practice witchcraft, destroy capitalism, and become lesbians."
—Pat Robertson, campaigning in Iowa to defeat State ERA

She Said:

"My only hope is that, one day soon, women, who have all earned their right to their opinions, instead of being labeled opinionated, will be called smart and well-informed, just like men."
—Teresa Heinz Kerry, philanthropist

 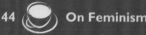

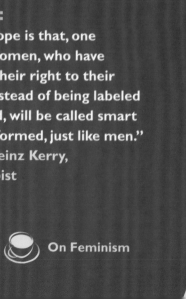

He Said:

"Football is a game played with arms, legs, and shoulders, but mostly from the neck up."

—Knute Rockne, football coach

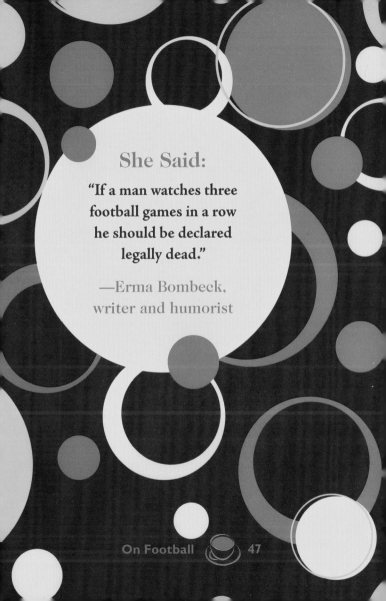

She Said:

"If a man watches three football games in a row he should be declared legally dead."

—Erma Bombeck, writer and humorist

He Said:

"Give a woman a job and she grows balls."
—Jack Gelber, playwright

She Said:

"There are very few jobs that require a penis or vagina. All other jobs ought to be open to everybody."
—Florynce Kennedy, lawyer and activist

He Said:

"Gossip is a vice enjoyed vicariously."
—Elbert Hubbard,
writer and philosopher

She Said:

"I don't call it gossip.
I call it 'emotional speculation.'"
—Laurie Colwin, author

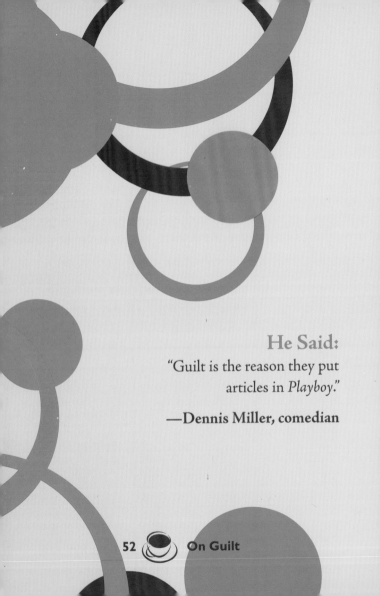

He Said:
"Guilt is the reason they put
articles in *Playboy*."

—Dennis Miller, comedian

She Said:
"Guilt is the price we pay willingly for doing what we are going to do anyway."

—Isabelle Holland, writer

 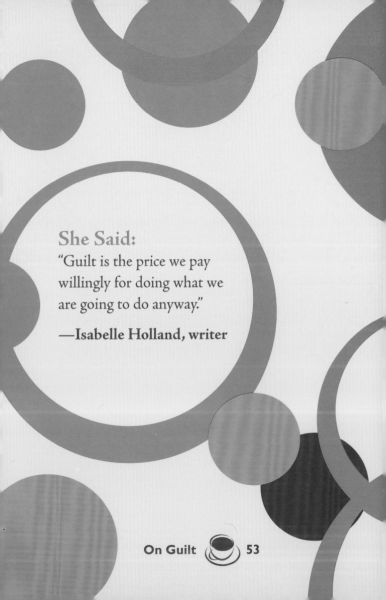

he said

"Fundamental happiness depends more than anything else upon what may be called a friendly interest in persons and things."

—Bertrand Russell, philosopher and Nobel Laureate

  On Happiness

"We have lived through the era when happiness was a warm puppy, and the era when happiness was a dry martini, and now we have come to the era when happiness is knowing what your uterus looks like."

—Nora Ephron, essayist, novelist, screenwriter, and director

she said

"In heaven, all the interesting people are missing."

—Friedrich Nietzsche, philosopher

she said "My idea of heaven is a big baked potato and someone to share it with." —Oprah Winfrey, media personality, magazine publisher, and philanthropist

He Said:

"The obvious and fair solution to the housework problem is to let men do the housework for, say, the next six thousand years, to even things up."

—Dave Barry, humorist

She Said:

"Housekeeping
ain't no joke!"

—Louisa May Alcott, author

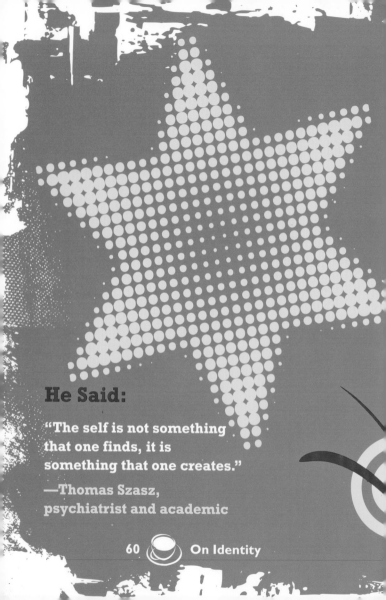

He Said:

"The self is not something that one finds, it is something that one creates."

—Thomas Szasz,
psychiatrist and academic

She Said:

"I feel there are two people inside me—me and my intuition. If I go against her, she'll screw me every time, and if I follow her, we get along quite nicely."

—Kim Basinger, actress

"Never tell people how to do things. Tell them what to do and they will surprise you with their ingenuity."

—George S. Patton Jr.,
U.S. Army General

On Leadership

"The trouble with talking nicely is that, unfortunately, some people don't hear you until you scream."

—Stefanie Powers, actress

He Said:

"All life is the progression towards, and the recession from, one phrase— I love you."

—F. Scott Fitzgerald, author

She Said:

"The word love has by no means the same sense for both sexes, and this is the cause of the serious misunderstandings that divide them."

—Simone de Beauvoir, author

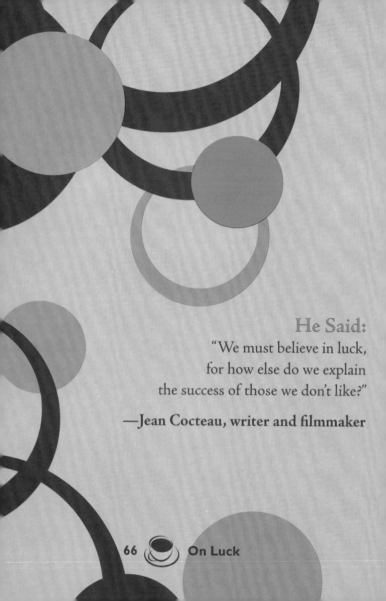

He Said:
"We must believe in luck,
for how else do we explain
the success of those we don't like?"

—Jean Cocteau, writer and filmmaker

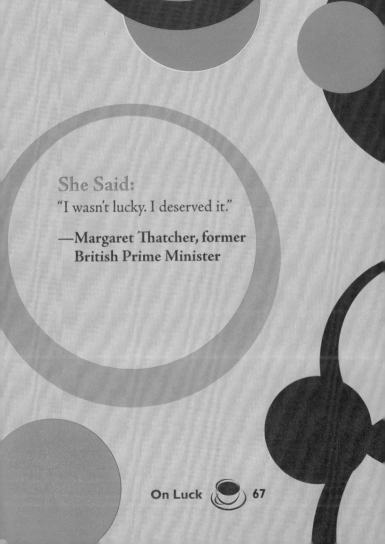

She Said:

"I wasn't lucky. I deserved it."

—Margaret Thatcher, former British Prime Minister

He Said:

"Women marry men hoping they will change. Men marry women hoping they will not. So each is inevitably disappointed."

—Albert Einstein,
scientist and Nobel Laureate

"Women's total
instinct for gambling
is satisfied by
marriage."

—Gloria Steinem,
author and activist

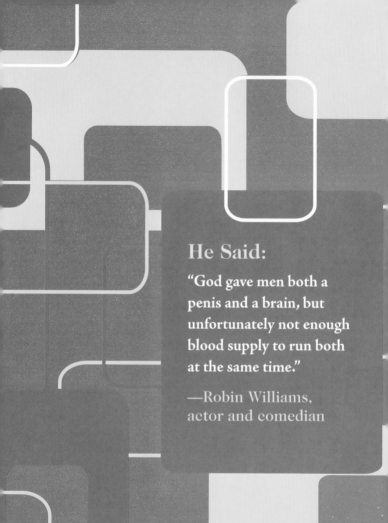

He Said:

"God gave men both a penis and a brain, but unfortunately not enough blood supply to run both at the same time."

—Robin Williams, actor and comedian

She Said:

"I require only three things of a man: He must be handsome, ruthless, and stupid."

—Dorothy Parker, writer and poet

"Money and women. They're two of the strongest things in the world. The things you do for a woman you wouldn't do for anything else. Same with money."

—Satchel Paige,
pitcher for Negro League
and Major League baseball

"Women who pay their own rent don't have to be nice."

—Katharine Dunn,
writer

she said

He Said:

"No matter how happily a woman may be married, it always pleases her to discover that there is a nice man who wishes that she were not."
—H. L. Mencken, writer and editor

She Said:

"Mind you, I'm not a monogamist in theory, only in practice."
—Zelda Fitzgerald, Jazz Age personality

He Said:

"Passion makes the world go round. Love just makes it a safer place."

—**Ice T, rap musician and actor**

"Jump out the window if you are the object of passion. Flee it if you feel it. Passion goes, boredom remains."

—Coco Chanel, fashion designer

He Said:

"All we are saying
is give peace a chance."
— John Lennon, musician

She Said:

"It isn't enough to talk about peace. One must
believe in it. And it isn't enough to believe in it.
One must work at it."
— Eleanor Roosevelt,
former First Lady of the United States

He Said:

"I worked with Freud in Vienna. We broke over the concept of penis envy. Freud thought it should be limited to women."

—Leonard Zelig, character and director's alter ego in Woody Allen film *Zelig*

She Said:

"I wonder why men can get serious at all. They have this delicate, long thing hanging outside their bodies, which goes up and down by its own will . . . If I were a man I would always be laughing at myself."

—Yoko Ono, artist and activist

He Said:

"[The advancement of women into the Senate] is one of the best changes of my career. They're smart, and we like to look at them."

—Strom Thurmond, United States Senator

She Said:

"When men in politics are together, testosterone poisoning makes them insane."

—Peggy Noonan, political commentator and author

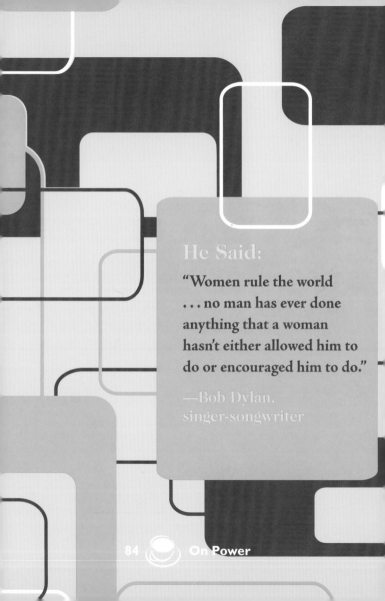

He Said:

"Women rule the world . . . no man has ever done anything that a woman hasn't either allowed him to do or encouraged him to do."

—Bob Dylan, singer-songwriter

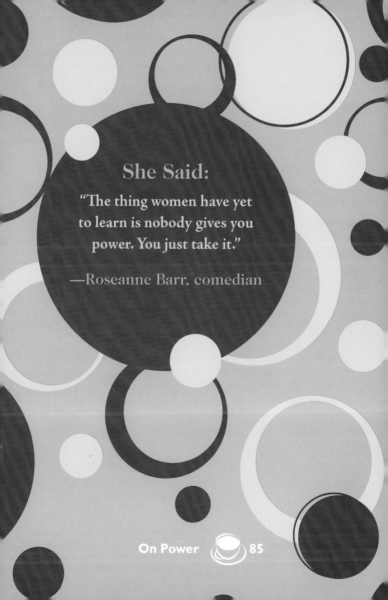

She Said:

"The thing women have yet to learn is nobody gives you power. You just take it."

—Roseanne Barr, comedian

"*Motherhood is never honored by excessive talk about the heroics of pregnancy.*"

—Leonard Feeney, conservative Roman Catholic theologian

she said "If men had to have babies, they would only ever have one each." —Diana, Princess of Wales

He Said:

"The greatest and most important
problems in life are all
in a certain sense insoluble."

—Carl Jung, psychotherapist

She Said:

"There must be quite a few things a hot bath won't cure, but I don't know many of them."

—Sylvia Plath, poet

"Winning isn't everything—it's the only thing."

—Vince Lombardi,
football coach

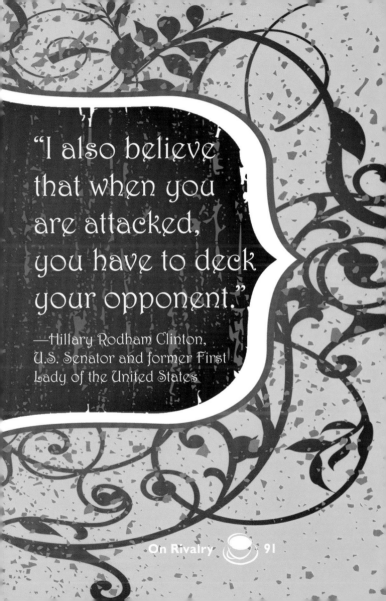

"I also believe that when you are attacked, you have to deck your opponent."

—Hillary Rodham Clinton, U.S. Senator and former First Lady of the United States

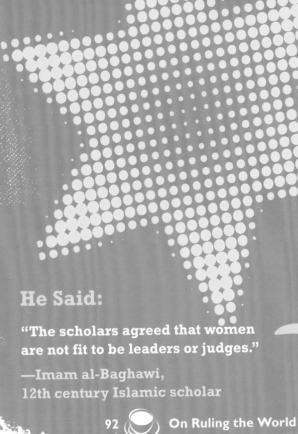

He Said:

"The scholars agreed that women are not fit to be leaders or judges."

—Imam al-Baghawi,
12th century Islamic scholar

She Said:

"I've had the same goal I've had ever since I was a girl. I want to rule the world."

—Madonna,
dance-pop singer-songwriter

He Said:

"Sex hasn't been
the same since women started
enjoying it."

—Lewis Grizzard, writer and humorist

"'Easy' is an adjective used to describe a woman who has the sexual morals of a man."

—Nancy Linn-Desmond, author

He Said:

"I buy women shoes and they use them to walk away from me."
—Mickey Rooney, actor

She Said:

"If she never takes off her high-heeled shoes, how will she ever know how far she could walk or how fast she could run?
—Germaine Greer, author and activist

he said

"Virtue we still consider the best goal for others: but for ourselves, success."

—E. V. Lucas, essayist

"The worst part of success is to try to find someone who is happy for you."

—Bette Midler,
actress and singer

He Said:

"Yes, risk-taking is inherently failure-prone. Otherwise, it would be called sure-thing-taking."

—Jim McMahon, football player

She Said:

"What you risk reveals what you value."

—Jeanette Winterson, writer

He Said:

"One should always have one's boots on and be ready to leave."

—Michel de Montaigne,
French Renaissance essayist

On Travel

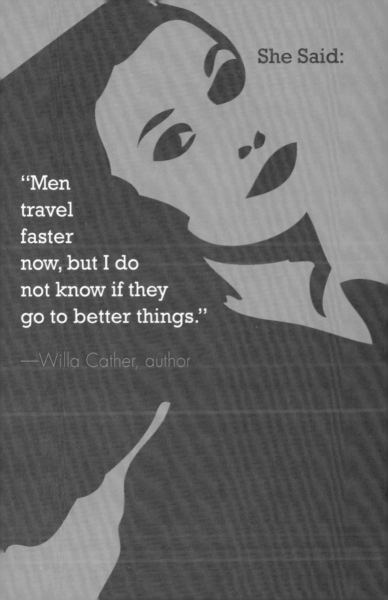

She Said:

"Men travel faster now, but I do not know if they go to better things."

—Willa Cather, author

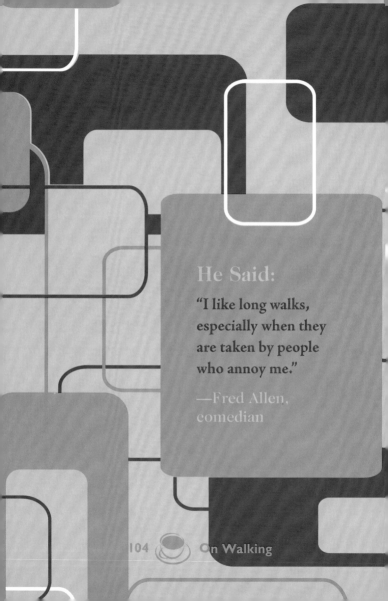

He Said:

"I like long walks, especially when they are taken by people who annoy me."

—Fred Allen, comedian

She Said:

"My grandmother started walking five miles a day when she was sixty. She's ninety-seven today and we don't know where the hell she is."

—Ellen DeGeneres, comedian and talk-show host

"You only require two things in life: your sanity and your wife."

—Tony Blair,
former British Prime Minister

she said "Sitting around the house playing the wife and mother is driving me crazy." —Patsy Cline, country singer

He Said:

"The great question that has never been answered, and which I have not yet been able to answer, despite my thirty years of research into the feminine soul, is 'What does a woman want?'"
—Sigmund Freud, psychoanalyst

She Said:

"Women want mediocre men and men are working to be as mediocre as possible."
—Margaret Mead, anthropologist

He Said:

"Work is the refuge of people who have nothing better to do."

—Oscar Wilde,
poet, playwright, and wit

On Work

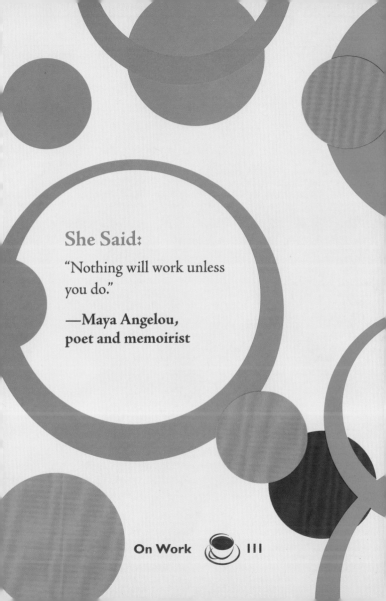

She Said:

"Nothing will work unless you do."

—Maya Angelou, poet and memoirist